Heroes of the Revolution

George Washington

By Susan & John Lee

Illustrated by Richard Wahl

 CHILDRENS PRESS, CHICAGO

Library of Congress Cataloging in Publication Data

Lee, Susan.
  George Washington.

  (Heroes of the Revolution)
  SUMMARY: An easy-to-read biography of the United
States' first President.
  1. Washington, George, Pres. U.S., 1732-1799—
Juvenile literature. [1. Washington, George, Pres.
U.S., 1732-1799. 2. Presidents] I. Lee, John,
joint author. II. Wahl, Richard, 1939-   illus.
III. Title.
E312.66.L43   973.4'1'0924 [B] [92]   74-8964
ISBN 0-516-04654-3

1 2 3 4 5 6 7 8 9 10 11 12 13 14 15 16 17 18 19 20 21 22 23 24 25 R 75 74

People like to tell stories about great men and women. Some of these stories are true. Some of these stories are called tall tales.

A tall tale is a story that makes a person seem taller . . . or braver . . . or stronger . . . than a person could have been. Tall tales often sound like true stories. But tall tales are not true stories.

One of the tall tales about George Washington goes like this: When George was a boy, he took a hatchet and cut down one of his father's cherry trees.

When George's father saw the tree, he asked, "Who cut down my cherry tree?"

"We don't know who did it," said the workers.

That night, George's father asked George, "Do you know who cut down my cherry tree?"

George just stood there. He didn't say anything.

"Do you know, son?" asked his father.

Then George said, "I did it, father. I cannot tell a lie. I cut down your cherry tree."

This story is a tall tale. George didn't cut down his father's cherry tree. Someone made up that story. People like the story because it shows that George was very honest.

History is full of tall tales. People like stories about heroes. We look up to our heroes. Heroes do things we like. Why do you think people made up tall tales about George Washington?

George Washington was born in a colony called Virginia. At that time, there was no United States of America. There were 13 colonies along the Atlantic Ocean. These colonies belonged to England. Their king was the King of England.

George's mother and father were English colonists. A colonist was a person living in a colony. The colonists in Virginia were Englishmen and Englishwomen. They lived under English law and called England their "mother country."

Virginia was one of England's richest
colonies. The colonists of Virginia made
money growing tobacco and rice. They
farmed the land along the rivers that ran
into the Atlantic Ocean. George's father
owned many farms. He had slaves who
helped him work his land.

George learned to read and write. He was very good in arithmetic. He liked numbers. Two and two were always four. Ten and ten were always twenty. George liked things that came out right every time.

George was a strong boy, and big for his age. He did not have much work on the farm. The slaves did most of the work. George had lots of time to play. He liked to shoot and hunt. He liked horses and was a good rider.

As a young man, George made plans for the kind of work he would do. He needed to make money. One way to make money is to know how to do something others cannot do for themselves.

George was good at arithmetic. So he picked a job where arithmetic was needed. When people own land, they need to know how much land they have. They need to know the shape of their land. They want a map of their land. A person who can make this kind of map is called a surveyor.

George went to work for a surveyor.
Before long, he could tell the size and
shape of a person's land. He learned to
make maps. Soon George was getting good
money for his work.

When George was 16, he got his first big job. Some men were going into the wilderness. They were going to survey the land. They would make many maps. Then people could move into this land and farm it. The men asked George to come along. He would work as a surveyor.

George was away from home for over a month. It rained a lot and he was often wet. He worked hard and he was often tired. One night his tent blew down. Another night a fire started in the straw where George was sleeping. Sometimes the group had no food. George found out how hard it was to hunt in the wilderness.

One day the men ran into a group of 30 Indians. The Indians and the surveyors were friendly with each other. George had never seen so many Indians in one place. He could not take his eyes off them.

The Indians made a big fire. One took a
pot and put a deer skin over it. He began to
beat his homemade drum. Then some of
the Indians began to dance around the fire.
George wrote down all that he saw. When
he got home he told his brothers and sisters
about the Indians and the land in the
wilderness.

News about the good wilderness land got around fast. Many English colonists began to move west with their families. They wanted to farm these rich lands. They wanted to buy their own farms, not work for someone else.

Soon, trouble began. Colonists from France liked the wilderness too. They trapped furs in the hills and by the small rivers. They made money by trading with the Indians.

It wasn't long before the French and the English began to fight. You can't farm and trap for fur on the same lands. England said the land was theirs. France said the land was theirs. No one asked the Indians who the land belonged to.

The French moved some soldiers into the wilderness. The English king sent an army to Virginia to fight the French. By 1756 the French and English were at war.

George Washington wanted to help
England win the war. He knew his way
around the wilderness. He was known as a
brave man. When he was only 23, he
became head of all the Virginia soldiers.

George was a good soldier. He showed
the English soldiers and the colonists how
to fight Indians. He helped build forts in
the wilderness to keep the French out.

George was glad when the French lost the war. He had done a good job in the army. The colonists said he was a good soldier. The English said he was a brave soldier.

Soon after he left the army, George married Martha Custis. For the next few years, George was busy with his home, called Mount Vernon. He bought more lands to farm. He owned land near the ocean and some in the wilderness. George did well as a farmer.

George grew into a fine man. The people who lived near him liked him. They picked him to work in the Virginia government as a lawmaker.

The Washingtons had many friends. George and Martha liked to play cards, dance, and talk with their neighbors. There was no more trouble with the French. It looked as if peace had come at last to Virginia.

This peace did not last long. Soon after the war was over, more trouble began. The English wanted the colonists to help pay for the war with France. They wanted to get money by taxing the colonists.

The colonists did not like the new taxes. They said the "mother country" had no right to make the colonists pay these taxes. When the taxes went on anyway, the colonists did not pay them. They got very mad at the King.

The people of Boston, Massachusetts, made the biggest fuss. They would not pay taxes on English tea. They would not buy English goods. The King sent soldiers to stop the trouble in Boston. The people called the soldiers "Redcoats" and other names. They wanted the soldiers to go home.

The Redcoats did not leave Boston. The men of Massachusetts began to practice with their guns. They got together and practiced marching. These men were called "Minute Men" because they could get ready to fight in a minute's time.

Then, on April 19, 1775, fighting began. English soldiers and Massachusetts Minute Men started shooting at each other. The people of Massachusetts asked other colonies to help them. In all the colonies people were asking, "Should we go to war with England?"

A few weeks later, men from 12 of the 13 colonies held a meeting in Philadelphia. The meeting was called a Congress. The men who came to the Congress were the leaders picked by the people of their colony. Benjamin Franklin was there. So was John Hancock and Thomas Jefferson. George Washington was one of the men sent from Virginia.

The men at the Congress said that the colonies should fight England. They started an army and asked the colonists to join. Then they needed someone to lead the soldiers.

The men of the Congress had heard of Washington's bravery. They knew he had fought well in the war with France. Everyone at the meeting picked George Washington to head the new army. George said he would serve as general without pay. He had fought the French. Now he would fight the English!

The first thing General Washington did was go to Massachusetts. There he took over the Minute Men who had been fighting the English soldiers. For eight months Washington and his men kept the Redcoats trapped in Boston.

At last, the English general decided to leave Boston. In March of 1776 the English sailed away and the American Army marched into the city. The colonists began to think they could win.

Then the Congress in Philadelphia voted for a Declaration of Independence from England. The Declaration said that the colonies were free and independent states. When General Washington read the Declaration to his soldiers, they yelled, "Three cheers for freedom!"

Washington knew that independence had to be won from England. It would not be easy. The English would not give up their colonies without a fight. Americans would have to fight to be free.

General Washington took his army from Boston to New York. The King was sending ship after ship of English soldiers across the Atlantic. The small army of Americans was no match for them. The English won a battle and took New York City. General Washington was in danger of being caught. He marched his men south and crossed the Delaware River into Pennsylvania.

The English general and his men
couldn't follow Washington. The English
didn't have any boats to cross the Delaware
River. As winter came, Washington
watched the weather every day. He knew if
it got very cold, the river would turn to ice.
Then the English soldiers could walk
across the river and fight the Americans.
But December came, and the Delaware
River did not turn to ice.

Then General Washington made a new plan. He would attack the English camp at Trenton. He would do it on a holiday. He had lots of small boats. If he took his men across the Delaware River at night, no one would see him coming. The English soldiers would not be looking for him on a holiday. It was a good plan.

General Washington waited until Christmas. That night, his soldiers left camp and got into small boats. Crossing the Delaware River was not easy. Big pieces of ice hit the boats. The wind made it hard to row across the river. It was three in the morning before all the soldiers got across the river.

Trenton was still nine miles away. A heavy
snow began to fall as Washington's men
started their long march. The muddy roads
made it hard to walk. It was daylight before
they got to the English camp.

The Americans caught the King's men by surprise. Washington saw that the English soldiers were in a trap. They fought back for awhile, but it was no use. After an hour, the English gave up. The Americans had won! Now, Trenton became an American camp.

The fight at Trenton did not end the
war. In September of 1777, the English
fought Washington near Philadelphia and
won. Hundreds of English soldiers
marched into Philadelphia. The men of
Congress had to run for their lives.

Washington tried to win back the city.
But it was no use. The English had more
men and guns. Washington could not drive
the English out of Philadelphia.

General Washington had to find a place for his soldiers to spend the winter. The camp he picked was called Valley Forge. Nearby were trees for making fires and building huts. There were also streams so the men could have water.

The winter was a very hard one for the American army. Some men had no coats. Many men had no shoes and wore rags on their feet. Weeks went by and the soldiers got no pay. Some men left the camp. As the new year came, Washington did not know if he could keep his little army together.

Washington's men almost died. It snowed so much that horses could not bring food to Valley Forge. Soon the meat and bread were gone. The men went without food for over a week.

Washington did not want his men to die of hunger. But he would not give up. His wife Martha came to be with him, and she took care of sick soldiers. Washington was as bad off as his men. The soldiers said they could take anything their general could. The men hung on until the food got to them.

With spring came good news. France wanted the American colonies to win independence. The French king would go to war with England once again. He would send ships and soldiers to help the Americans.

When the men at Valley Forge heard this news, they cried, "Long live the King of France!" Washington called for a day of thanksgiving. The soldiers marched in front of their general. They shot off 13 guns — one for each of the 13 new states. Washington was sure he could win the war with French help.

In the next two years, the English won some battles. The Americans won some. Then, in August of 1781, the English general, Lord Cornwallis, took his army to Yorktown, Virginia. This was a bad move for the English.

By September, the Americans and French were ready to trap Cornwallis. French ships sailed up the York River so the English could not get away by water. At the same time, General Washington put American and French soldiers all around the city. Lord Cornwallis saw no way to get out of the trap. In a few weeks, he and his 7,000 men gave up. With France's help, America had won the war!

British Fleet

Washington

French Fleet

YORKTOWN

The winning of independence made George Washington a hero. His soldiers loved him for his bravery. They loved him because he loved America. The soldiers had tears in their eyes when Washington said good-bye to them. The men of Congress thanked him for what he and his soldiers had done. As he rode to Mount Vernon, George Washington waved his hat at the people who cheered him.

For the rest of his life, George Washington helped his country in many ways. He helped write the Constitution. He was the first President of the United States. For eight years, President Washington worked to give the United States a good start. At the end of his life, Washington set all his slaves free.

As soon as Washington died, people began to tell tall tales about him. They wanted a hero they could look up to. But a story is just a story. George Washington does not need tall tales about his life. The true things he did were enough to make him a great American.

About the Authors:

Susan Dye Lee has been writing professionally since she graduated from college in 1961. Working with the Social Studies Curriculum Center at Northwestern University, she has created course materials in American studies. Ms. Lee has also co-authored a text on Latin America and Canada, written case studies in legal history for the Law in American Society Project, and developed a teacher's guide for tapes that explore women's role in America's past. The writer credits her students for many of her ideas. Currently, she is doing research for her history dissertation on the Women's Christian Temperance Union for Northwestern University. In her free moments, Susan Lee enjoys traveling, playing the piano, and welcoming friends to "Highland Cove," the summer cottage she and her husband, John, share.

John R. Lee enjoys a prolific career as a writer, teacher, and outdoorsman. After receiving his doctorate in social studies at Stanford, Dr. Lee came to Northwestern University's School of Education, where he advises student teachers and directs graduates in training. A versatile writer, Dr. Lee has co-authored the Scott-Foresman social studies textbooks for primary-age children. In addition, he has worked on the production of 50 films and over 100 filmstrips. His biographical film on Helen Keller received a 1970 Venice Film Festival award. His college text, *Teaching Social Studies in the Elementary School*, has recently been published. Besides pro-football, Dr. Lee's passion is his Wisconsin Cottage, where he likes to shingle leaky roofs, split wood, and go sailing.

About the Artist:

Richard Wahl received his B.A. from Kentucky Wesleyan College, and his B.F.A. from the Art Center College of Design in Los Angeles. Since then he has illustrated many books and magazine articles. Richard is a skilled artist and photographer who advocates realistic interpretations of his subjects. He lives with his wife and two sons in Libertyville, Illinois.